DO YOU KNOW THE NAMES OF GOD?

Quiz Part 2

By

Paul Muinde

(Elder Shalom)

Table of Contents

DO YOU KNOW THE NAMES OF GOD?	1
Copyright Information	4
Introduction	5
The Personal Name of God	8
God With Us (Immanuel)	11
How To Use The Rest Of This Book	15
1. The LORD Our Righteousness	15
2. The God Who is There	19
3. The Lord Our Sanctifier	22
4. The Lord of Hosts	24
5. The God of Our Salvation	26
6. The Lord My Rock	29
7. The Lord My Strength	31
8. The Lord My Light	33
9. The Lord Our Great Reward	36
10. The Lord Our Refuge	38
11. The Lord Our Shield	40
12. The Lord My God My King	42
13. The Forgiving God	44
14. The God Who Performs	46
15. The Lord God Of Knowledge	48
16. The Lord The Awesome God	50
17. The God of Truth	52
18. The Merciful God	55
19. The God of Compassion	58
20. The Gracious God	61

Answers & Prayers Using the Names of God   64
Further Reading   88
About the Author   89

Do You Know The Names of God? Part 2

Copyright Information

Copyright 2014 Paul Muinde

Introduction

This is Book 2 in the series on the names of God. Book 1 covered 20 Hebrew names of God. Book 2 covers some other 20 names. In order to have a right perspective of the names here is the introduction once more.

God's names came through revelation to His people. God used them to reveal His character and nature to the nation of Israel. These names are compound names and they are meant to be descriptive. God created intimacy with the nation of Israel through these revelations.

The nation of Israel would call upon God using specific names in different situations for God to manifest Himself according to the way He had described Himself. The names are transliterated from the Hebrew language into the English alphabet. There are several renderings of some of the names e.g. Yahweh Sabaoth is commonly written as Yahweh Tsebaoth.

The Bible tells us to give thanks and call upon the name of the Lord (Psalm 105:1a) and to make His deeds known. It also says that His name is excellent in all the earth (Psalm 8:9). God makes a promise to promote or to set on high those who have known His name (Psalm 91:14b).

At the "burning bush" God had described Himself to Moses as the God of his father, the God of Abraham, of Isaac and of Jacob (Exodus 3:6). When God was sending Moses to deliver the nation of Israel from bondage in Egypt, Moses asked for God's name so that he could tell the Israelites who had sent him. God told him to say "I AM" or "I AM THAT I AM" had sent him (Exodus 3:14). In Hebrew it is " Ehyeh-Asher-Ehyeh". This has been interpreted in a number of ways. One of them is that God never changes.

God is the same always – hence the present tense. It is also a tautology like 1=1. Since God is infinite it is not fully possible to describe Him. That is why in most cases He reveals Himself by His personal name (Yahweh or Jehovah) followed by an attribute of His character. His personal name as you will see later is derived from the Hebrew verb "to be".

In Hebrew El (capital E) stands for God (capital G) but el (lowercase e) stands for god (lowercase g). There are many constructs of Yahweh's name with the word "El" e.g. Yahweh El Elyon which means "Yahweh God Most High".

This quiz book series is to help Christians and others who share the Old Testament to meditate on the names of God and know them by heart. This will help believers in their worship of the True and Living God, Yahweh.

In order to gain the most from the quiz, it is necessary to memorize a few names per day e.g. pick three names and meditate on them during the day. Start with those that seem to be familiar or close to your heart. Within a short time, you will know many of them.

During your fellowship with God, start referring to Him by His names and your worship and fellowship will grow richer day by day. Apply His name to your situations. For example when you are in need, worship and acknowledge Yahweh as your Yahweh Yireh (your provider) or Yahweh El Shaddai (your sufficiency). Likewise when you feel lost acknowledge Him as Yahweh Rohi (your Shepherd).

Shalom.

Do You Know The Names of God? Part 2

The Personal Name of God

God has a personal or proper name. It is represented by four Hebrew letters:

This is known as the Tetragrammaton. It is derived from a Hebrew verb "to be".

Hebrew letter	ה	ו	ה	י
Name of letter	He	Waw (sometimes written Vav)	He	Yodh
English letter	H	W	H	Y

Hebrew is read from right to left but English is from left to right, so the name is transliterated to YHWH in English commonly pronounced and even written as Yahweh. This is often seen as a blend between two names YHWH and Hashem (the Name) from which the "a" and "e" are derived. The Jews avoid mentioning or writing the name in full for fear of using it in vain or in blasphemy so they often use Hashem instead.

The third commandment in Exodus 20:7 is that "You shall not take the name of Jehovah (some versions use the LORD) your God in vain. For Jehovah (the LORD) will not hold him guiltless that takes His name in vain." (MKJV)

Because of this fear the Jews preferred to use the name Adon (or Adonai) which means LORD (or my LORD) instead of YHWH. All capital letters were used to avoid confusing it with other types of lords. Thus it appears in some Bible translations (versions) in this form. It stands for sovereign owner of everything. The name "God" is also used, interchangeably, in English Bibles.

It should be noted that YHWH was also transliterated into JHVH from which Jehovah was derived. However it should be noted that the letter "J" in Hebrew is actually pronounced as "Y". It is recorded that the form "Jehovah" started appearing in English Bibles after the 16th century. The 1611 KJV Bible uses the following spellings "IEHOVAH" and "Iehouah" for YHWH. Some scholars therefore recommend the use of YHWH or Yahweh instead.

Psalm 83:8

.. So that men may know that Your name is JEHOVAH (YHWH or Yahweh), that You alone are the Most High over all the earth. (MKJV)

God With Us (Immanuel)

One of the names God used prophesying the coming of Jesus Christ the Messiah (*Yeshua Hamashiac* in Hebrew) is Immanuel. The Prophet Isaiah prophesied the birth of Jesus Christ as Immanuel

*"Therefore the Lord himself shall give you a sign; Behold, a virgin shall conceive, and bear a son, and shall call his name **Immanuel** "* (Isaiah 7:14). The name means "God with us".

Because mankind had fallen into sin through Adam and Eve's disobedience to God's command in the Garden of Eden, God purposed to redeem mankind by visiting the earth Himself. He would be here on earth with us. That was His plan for mankind's salvation.

The angel of the LORD appeared to Mary and prophesied the birth of Jesus Christ as it is recorded in the Gospel of Luke:

*Luke 1:31 And behold! You shall conceive in your womb and bear a son, and you shall call His name **JESUS**.*

*Luke 1:32 He shall be great and shall be called the **Son of the Highest**. And the Lord God shall **give Him the throne of His father David**.*

*Luke 1:33 And He shall reign over the house of Jacob forever, and of **His kingdom there shall be no end.***

Luke 1:34 Then Mary said to the angel, How shall this be, since I do not know a man?

*Luke 1:35 And the angel answered and said to her, The Holy Spirit shall come on you, and the power of the Highest shall overshadow you. Therefore also that **Holy One** which will be born of you shall be called **Son of God**.*

Jesus Christ was the one prophesied about by Isaiah as Immanuel (God with us). God called Jesus Christ, His Son and gave Him the throne of David and declared that Jesus' reign shall never end. God had promised David many years ago that his throne would last forever.

2 Samuel 7:16 And your (David's) house and your kingdom shall be made sure forever before you. Your throne shall be established forever.

This was to be fulfilled through Jesus Christ who was a descendant of David since Mary was of the lineage of David but His Father is the Holy Spirit (God). Jesus qualified to redeem mankind. He entered the earth as a man even though He had the Spirit of God. He is the mediator between God and man. He is sometimes referred to as the God-man. He often referred to Himself the Son of Man.

Jesus responded to the Jews with these words:

John 8:58 "Jesus said to them, Truly, truly, I say to you, Before Abraham came into being, I AM!"(MKJV)

The Bible tells us in Romans 11:33

"O the depth of the riches both of the wisdom and knowledge of God; how unsearchable are His judgments and His ways past finding out."

God uses His own counsel (advice) i.e. He advises Himself. For His salvation plan to work He had to enter the earth as a man. For mankind had fallen into sin through one man (Adam) so salvation was to come through one man, Jesus Christ the Messiah (*Yeshua Hamashiac* in Hebrew). *Yeshua* means salvation. Here is a historical summary:

1) Sin entered the world through Adam

Romans 5:12. Therefore, even as through one man sin entered into the world, and death by sin, and so death passed on all men inasmuch as all sinned:

Romans 5:14. But death reigned from Adam to Moses, even over those who had not sinned in the likeness of the transgression of Adam, who is the type of Him who was to come;

2) The wages of sin is death.

Romans 6:23. For the wages of sin is death, but the gift of God is eternal life through Jesus Christ our Lord.

3) Jesus Christ has reconciled us to God.

Romans 5:11. And not only so, but we also rejoice in God through our Lord Jesus Christ, by whom we have now received the reconciliation.

Romans 5:17. For if by one man's offense death reigned by one, much more they who receive abundance of grace and the gift of righteousness shall reign in life by One, Jesus Christ.

Now that we know the personal name of God and the fact that He came to the earth to reconcile mankind to Himself through Jesus Christ – the Messiah, we can now look at the descriptive names of God. These names are usually appended to His personal name to describe His character and His attributes.

How To Use The Rest Of This Book

For best results:

1. Read each chapter and meditate on it. Try to answer the question at the end of the chapter.

2. Check the answer.

3. Pray the prayer and ensure that you memorize the name and meditate on it.

4. You can limit the reading to three (3) names i.e. three chapters at a time.

5. At each reading session, you can start by trying to remember the names you have memorized so far. If you have forgotten, it is better to go back and memorize them before continuing.

6. Within a short time you will be able to remember all the twenty (20) names in this book. This will enrich your prayer life.

1. The LORD Our Righteousness

"WE ARE THE RIGHTEOUSNESS OF GOD IN CHRIST JESUS ON EARTH..."

What is righteousness? It is a state of having a right standing with someone. In this case we are talking of having a right standing with God. When Adam sinned in the Garden of Eden, he lost that righteousness. His relationship with God was cut off. God has principles which He lives by. He had told Adam that if Adam ate the fruit of the forbidden tree, Adam would die. This was both a spiritual death and a physical death. The word of God says "all have sinned and fallen short of the glory of God" (Rom. 3:23). Another portion of scripture states that "the wages of sin is death but the gift of God is eternal life through Jesus Christ our Lord" (Rom. 6:23).

Finally "all our righteousness is like filthy rags" (Isaiah 64:6). It means that however much we try to be right with God, we cannot base it on our own efforts. Since man could not achieve restoration of His fellowship with God on his own, God took the prerogative to restore the relationship and fellowship. We are saved by grace through in Jesus Christ. Salvation is a gift from God (Eph. 2:8-9). One has to accept and confess Jesus Christ as Lord and Savior (Rom. 10:9-10) and obey His commandments (John 14:21,23).

God, Himself, had to impart His own righteousness to us through His Son, Jesus Christ. Those who accept Jesus Christ as Lord and Savior receive God's righteousness as a gift.

An Old Testament prophet prophesied that a King would be born of the lineage of King David who would execute justice on earth and who would be called the LORD OUR RIGHTEOUSNESS. This was in reference to Jesus Christ, the Son of God.

Do You Know The Names of God? Part 2

Which name below describes God as our righteousness?

A) Yahweh Mekaddishkhem
B) Yahweh Tsidkenu
C) Yahweh El Gibbor

Check answer on **Page 65.**

2. The God Who is There

"HE WHO WAS, WHO IS & WHO WILL ALWAYS BE"

There are three types of people. There are those who believe in the existence of a supernatural being (God) who is responsible for the creation of life. There are others who deny the existence of God. These are called atheists. Finally there are those who neither believe in the existence of God nor deny His existence. These are called agnostics. You can say they are non-committal.

Some in the two last categories believe in the theory of evolution by Darwin and the "big bang" theory. However some of them are slowly shifting their position based on new evidence which supports the concept of intelligent design i.e. that the complexity of life draws from some intelligent design which in itself presupposes some intelligent designer. This is being resisted by some other scientists who have effectively made Darwinism the absolute "truth" and have refused to consider the notion of intelligent design.

Darwin, himself, gave the assumptions on which he based his theory. He even said that if contrary information was discovered then his theory (or portions of it) could be discounted.

New discoveries that show that man did not evolve from other similar species is being rejected by the "mainstream" even when DNA tests show that man has very little in common with such species (less than 2%).

The Bible describes those who do not acknowledge the existence of God as "fools". In Psalm 14:1 "The fool has said in his heart, there is no God." This is repeated in Psalm 53:1. The Bible also states that the beginning of all wisdom is the fear of God. This implies acknowledging Him and giving Him reverence. Proverbs 9:10 "The fear of Jehovah is the beginning of wisdom; and the knowledge of the holy is understanding."

Do You Know The Names of God? Part 2

Which name best describes God as the God who exists?

A) Yahweh Sali
B) Yahweh El Roi
C) Yahweh Shammah

Check answer on Page 67.

3. The Lord Our Sanctifier

"HE SANCTIFIES US WITH THE BLOOD OF JESUS & HIS TRUTH .."

Sanctification is the process of making something clean in a spiritual sense. Jesus Christ had an issue with the Pharisees when they emphasized outward cleanliness more than inner cleanliness. They had cast aspersions on the disciples of Jesus Christ who did not wash their hands before eating a meal as was the custom of the Jews. In Matthew 15:2-11 Jesus told the Pharisees what defiles a person is not what they eat but what comes from their mouth (i.e. from within their hearts).

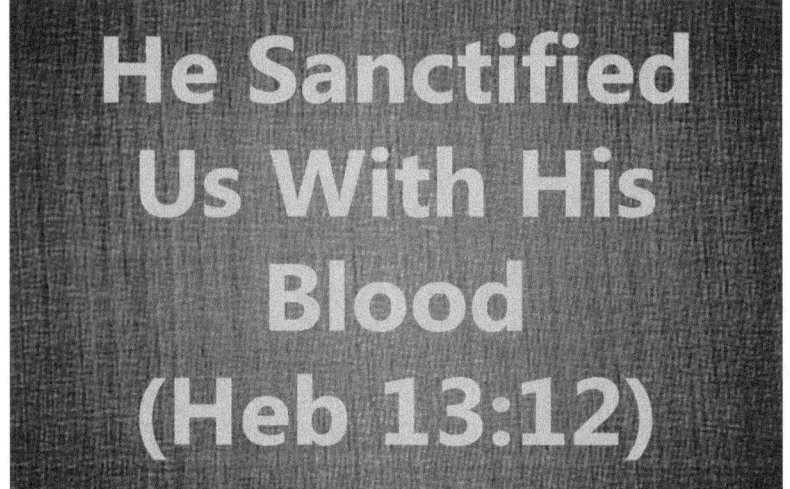

Jesus Christ prayed to the Father to sanctify the disciples through His Truth, which is His Word (John 17:17). Ephesians 5:26 states that Jesus sanctifies His Church by cleansing it with His Word. Finally, Hebrews 13:12 says "Therefore Jesus also, so that He might sanctify the people through His own blood, suffered outside the gate". Christians are sanctified by the blood of Jesus Christ and by His Word (the Truth).

Which name is used to describe God as the One who sanctifies?

A) Yahweh Mekaddishkem
B) Yahweh Tsidkenu
C) Yahweh El Olam

Check answer on Page 68.

4. The Lord of Hosts

"HE COMMANDS THE ARMIES OF HEAVEN"

In the Old Testament there are many battles that the nation of Israel had to fight, especially on their way to the land that God had promised Abraham. In many cases their armies were greatly outnumbered by the enemy, yet God (the Lord) gave them victory.

Most of the times they sought direction from the Lord before engaging in battle. In such cases, the Lord would confirm whether He would give them victory or not. When they assumed victory without consulting God, they would lose the battle (Joshua 7).

At one time they became over confident and relied on their numeric strength to wage war but God told Gideon to reduce the number of soldiers to only 300 before going to battle (Judges 7). He gave them victory to prove to them that it was not numeric strength but the fact that He fought for them that determined the outcome of the battle.

During one of the encounters, Israel had to fight three great armies. These were the Ammonites, the Moabites and those of mount Seir. It is recorded how God set an ambush against their enemies in 2 Chronicles 20:22

"And when they began to sing and to praise, Jehovah set ambushes against the sons of Ammon, Moab, and mount Seir, who had come against Judah. And they were beaten". (MKJV)

There is a specific name that refers to Yahweh as the Lord of Hosts (armies of Heaven). Which is it among the following?

A) Yahweh Tsebaoth
B) Yahweh Uzzi
C) Yahweh Shalom

Check answer on Page 69.

5. The God of Our Salvation

"SALVATION BELONGS TO OUR GOD.."

God has in many occasions appeared to those who call upon His name as the God who saves. This is evidenced in the history of the nation of Israel. He saved them from the slavery in Egypt. In the wilderness on their way to the Promised Land, He saved them from mighty armies. This salvation was linked to obedience to His Word. In fact, in addition to saving Israel from physical enemies, He would also save them from all diseases as long as they lived in obedience.

Deuteronomy 7:15 "And Jehovah will take away from you all sickness, and will put none of the evil diseases of Egypt which you know upon you. But He will lay them upon all who hate you". Deuteronomy 28:7 "Jehovah shall cause your enemies that rise up against you to be stricken before your face. They shall come out against you one way, and flee before you seven ways".

He Saved Us From Drowning in the Sea of Sin

Although God saves human beings from physical enemies, He is more interested in saving the souls of people. This latter salvation is not temporal (time-bound) but is eternal. The Old Testament speaks mainly about salvation from physical enemies but it also points to salvation of souls in the future. The New Testament reveals God's plan for the eternal salvation of mankind.

God's plan of salvation is revealed in John 3:16-17

"For God so loved the world that He gave His only-begotten Son, that whoever believes in Him should not perish but have everlasting life. (17) For God did not send His Son into the

world to condemn the world, but so that the world might be saved through Him".

Paul tells the Ephesians in Ephesians 2:8-9

"For by grace you are saved through faith, and that not of yourselves, it is the gift of God, (9) not of works, lest anyone should boast".

Which of the names of God best describes Him as the God of our Salvation?

A) Yahweh Mekaddishkhem
B) Yahweh El Olam
C) Yahweh El Yeshuatenu

Check answer on Page 70.

6. The Lord My Rock

"He is My Firm Foundation"

In the Bible a rock is used to signify a solid foundation and sometimes a place of refuge.

Isaiah 44:8 "'Do not tremble and do not be afraid; Have I not long since announced it to you and declared it? And you are My witnesses. Is there any God besides Me, Or is there any other Rock? I know of none.'"

2 Samuel 22:31-32 (Psalms 18:30-31) "As for God, His way is blameless; The word of the LORD is tested; He is a shield to all who take refuge in Him. "For who is God, besides the LORD? And who is a rock, besides our God?"

Jesus likened a person who hears God's Word and does it to the person who built his house on a rock. When the rains, the floods and winds came, his house remained secure (Matthew 7:24-27).

Jesus is also depicted as the rock which accompanied the children of Israel in their journey to the Promised Land as described in 1 Corinthians 10:4 " and all drank the same spiritual drink; for they drank of the spiritual Rock that followed them, and that Rock was Christ".

Which specific reference to God describes Him as the Rock?

A) Yahweh El Sali
B) Yahweh Rapha
C) Yahweh Megan

Check answer on Page 71.

7. The Lord My Strength

"He is My Strength in Hours of Weakness"

Paul's life was full of suffering but he had put his trust in God. He saw his weakness as an opportunity for God to manifest His strength as he writes in 2 Corinthians 12:9 "And He said to me, My grace is sufficient for you, for My power is made perfect in weakness.

Most gladly therefore I will rather glory in my weaknesses, that the power of Christ may overshadow me". In the Old Testament David often found himself surrounded by enemies. Sometimes even his friends turned against him and blamed him for some of the tragedies that befell them. He encouraged (comforted) himself in the Lord.

Psalm 22:19 "But You, O Jehovah, be not far from Me; O My strength, hurry to help Me!"

Psalm 28:7 "Jehovah is my strength and my shield; my heart trusted in Him, and I am helped; therefore my heart greatly rejoices; and with my song I will praise Him".

> **Be Strong in the LORD and in the Power of His Might (Ephesians 6:10)**

We can see that in both the Old and the New Testament, the servants of God depended on God for their strength.

Which name describes Yahweh as the God who is our strength?

A) Yahweh El Hannorah
B) Yahweh El Gomer
C) Yahweh Uzzi

Check answer on Page 72.

8. The Lord My Light

"I Walk In His Light"

Light has a lot of significance both in the spiritual and physical realms. The Word of God says in 1 John 1:5-7 that God is Light and in Him there is no darkness whatsoever. If we want to fellowship with Him and with other believers in the faith then we must walk in the light. The "light" is God's Word.

David testified that God's Word "is a lamp to my feet and a light to my path" Psalm 119:105. Another portion of scripture says "The entrance of God's Word gives light" Psalm 119:130. God is referred to as the Father of lights James 1:17. Jesus Christ called His disciples to be the light in the world.

Every born again person (practising Christian) has been delivered from the kingdom of darkness (Satan's kingdom) to the kingdom of light (the kingdom of God's dear Son - Jesus Christ). In the physical realm, science is catching up with God's Word and revealing the significance of light. Light is energy. It permeates the whole universe (except in black-holes in Space).

Time was previously perceived as a constant. It is no longer perceived as a constant in space-time. Time actually moves slower in moving objects. The interchange-ability of energy and matter is governed by the speed of light in Albert Einstein's equation ($E=mc2$).

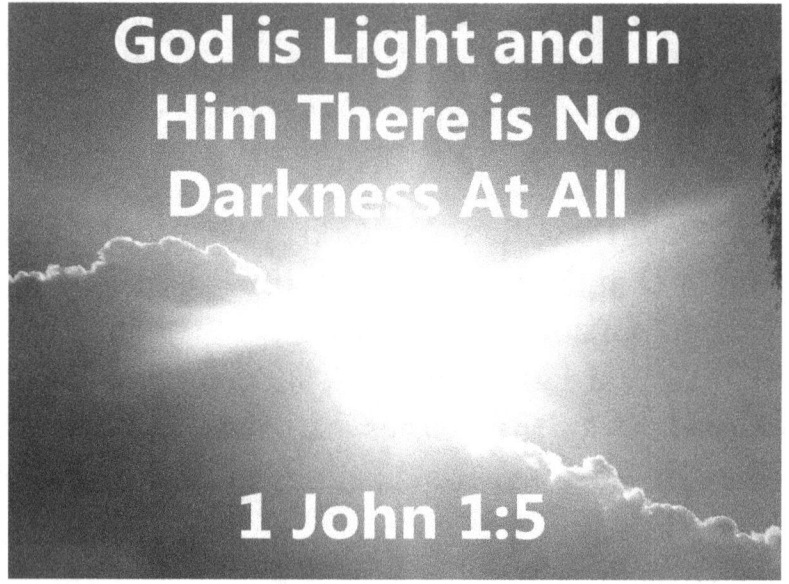

The Bible tells us that the earth was without form at some point in time after God created the heavens and the earth. Then God created light and order was realized. Thereafter the rest of creation was called to being. Finally, God said it was good (in order).

Which is the name of God that refers to Him as our Light?

A) Yahweh El Nose
B) Yahweh El Ganan
C) Yahweh Ori

Check answer on Page 73.

9. The Lord Our Great Reward

"HE REWARDS THOSE THAT DILIGENTLY SEEK HIM"

The Bible encourages believers not to lose hope or confidence in what they believe for God will reward those who do not give up. In Heb. 10:35 it says "Therefore do not cast away your confidence, which has great recompense of reward" (MKJV).

Christians often get discouraged in ministry as they serve. Sometimes the frustration is from other Christians and even Christian leaders who do not appreciate what they do. This discouragement sometimes causes divisions in churches. In Heb. 6:10-12, believers are told that God is not unrighteous to forget their diligent service.

They are told not to be slothful but to continue to the end for the promises of God are inherited (realized) through faith and patience as exemplified by the saints of old. Faith is a major component of a Christian's life. Without faith it is impossible to please God. Those who come to Him must first believe that He exists and that He rewards those who diligently seek Him (Heb 11:6). Those who have been justified (the just or righteous) are called to live by faith (Rom. 1:17, 2 Cor. 5:7).

1 Cor. 3:11-15 also encourages believers to build on the foundation that Jesus laid. Their service is categorized using different building materials such as gold, silver, precious stones, wood, hay and stubble. Everyone's work will be tested by fire at the end. Those whose work survives the fire will receive a reward.

Which of the descriptive names of God describes Him as the God who is our Great Reward?

A) Yahweh Emeth
B) Yahweh Rabah Sakar
C) Yahweh El Malki

Check answer on Page 74.

10. The Lord Our Refuge

"WE DWELL UNDER HIS SHADOW"

A refuge is a place of protection. The Psalmist in Psalm 46 from verse 1 states that God is our refuge and present help in times of trouble. Therefore whatever happens on earth, there is no need to fear. Again in Psalm 91:2 the Psalmist restates that God is his refuge. God is also his fortress and therefore he will put his trust in God.

In the previous verse Psalm 91:1 he talks of a secret place where he resides and where God covers him with God's shadow of protection. Life is full of challenges. There is really no safe place on the earth. There is insecurity in many parts of the world.

The frequency of natural calamities such as earthquakes, tornados and floods has also increased in the last 100 years. Even though most governments are doing their best to counter terrorism and other forms of insecurity and even forewarn populations of pending natural disasters, this is not adequate to address the challenges. Only God can intervene effectively for those who call upon Him and those who reverence Him.

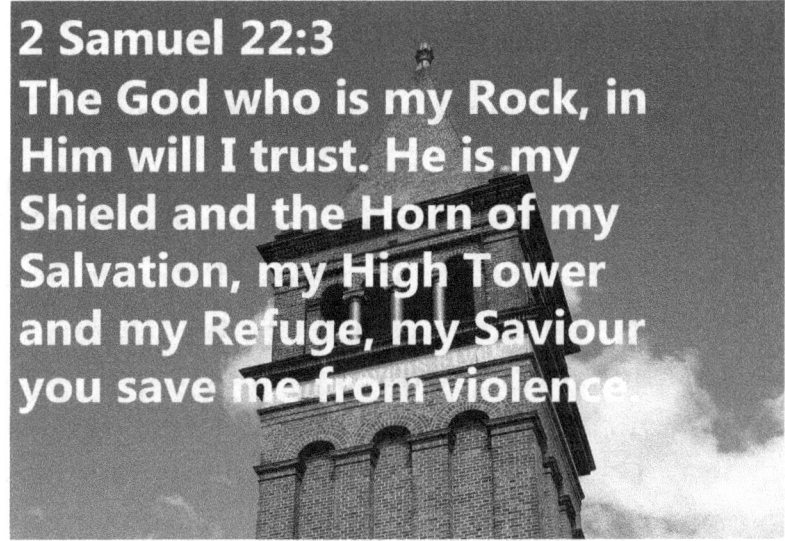

> 2 Samuel 22:3
> The God who is my Rock, in Him will I trust. He is my Shield and the Horn of my Salvation, my High Tower and my Refuge, my Saviour you save me from violence.

Christians need to pray always for God's protection. Jesus prayed for His disciples that they may be protected, not from natural disasters per se but from evil. The "Lord's Prayer" found in Matthew 6 is a model of how Christians ought to pray. Eph. 6:18 admonishes Christians to always pray with all manner of prayer in the spirit for all the saints.

Which of the descriptive names of God describes Him as the Lord our Refuge?

A) Yahweh Maxi (or Machsi)
B) Yahweh El Nose
C) Yahweh Uzzi

Check answer on Page 75.

11. The Lord Our Shield

"FOR HE IS OUR SHIELD AND DEFENDER"

A shield is a defensive weapon. In Eph. chapter 6 Christians are advised to wear the full armor of God. One of the pieces of the armor is the "Shield of Faith". This is used to thwart or divert the fiery darts of the evil one (devil). During the exodus of the Israelites from Egypt and their journey through the wilderness, God provided a shield for them (Exodus 13:21, 40:38). In addition to guiding them, this was to protect them from their enemies. He would provide a fire for this purpose at night. During the day He would shield them from the Sun by the cloud. The Psalmist said that God's truth was our shield.

Psalm 91:4-5 He shall cover you with His feathers, and under His wings you shall trust. His truth shall be your shield, and buckler. (5) You shall not fear the terror by night; nor because of the arrow that flies by day;

God has also declared that He would surround the righteous with favor as a shield in Psalm 5:12.

Which of the following names identifies God as our Shield?

A) Yahweh Ganan
B) Yahweh El Emeth
C) Yahweh Megan (Magen)

Check answer on Page 76.

12. The Lord My God My King

"He's King of Kings & Lord of Lords"

Jesus is referred to in the Bible as the King of kings and Lord of lords (1 Timothy 6:15, Rev. 17:14, Rev. 19:16). Jesus is the divine expression of the Father in bodily form (Hebrews 1:3, Colossians 2:9). The Bible says in whom the fullness of God dwelt bodily. When Philip the disciple asked Jesus to show them the Father, Jesus said to him, "Have I been with you such a long time and yet you have not known Me, Philip? He who has seen Me has seen the Father. And how do you say, Show us the Father?" John 14:9. God is Spirit. He manifested Himself to mankind in a body (flesh and blood) in the form Jesus Christ.

A king is not elected. He is normally appointed by a higher authority or inherits a kingdom. In the case of Israel the first king and the second were appointed by God. It is also possible for someone to impose himself as king by overthrowing the current king. This is what Absalom wanted to do but he failed to overthrow David, his father. A king owns everything in his kingdom. This means the king has sovereignty over the whole territory.

The people and their property belong to the king. The people are subjects of the king. This also means that the king has the responsibility to care, provide for and protect the people (his subjects). Whenever they have a need, they can call out to the king. Good kings ensure that there is provision and protection in their kingdom.

Which of the following names identifies God as my King? (Click the correct answer)

A) Yahweh El Kanno
B) Yahweh El Malki
C) Yahweh Ebenezer

Check answer on Page 77.

13. The Forgiving God

"HE IS RICH IN MERCY"

God is full of mercy. The Bible tells us that His mercies endure forever for those who fear Him and keep His commandments. The fear mentioned is reverence i.e. utmost respect. God's mercies are new every morning and He crowns us with His tender mercies and loving kindness (Psalm 103:4).

When people sin they can come to Him for forgiveness. However He cannot be fooled. There are people whose conscious has become dull and eventually becomes dead if they do not repent in good time. They believe that they can sin however much they want and ask for forgiveness from God because He is full of love and mercy.

God calls upon us to be holy because He is holy (1 Pet. 1:16). We are His offspring born of His Spirit to be a new creation, a royal priesthood, a holy nation, a peculiar people (1 Pet. 2:9). However if we happen to sin, accidentally or unwillingly, we can always call upon Him for forgiveness in the name of Jesus Christ. Jesus is our High Priest and advocate before our heavenly Father (1 Jn. 2:1). The Bible warns those who sin wilfully of dire consequences. There is no longer any other hope for them because they have rubbished their salvation (Heb. 10:26-29). They are like a dog returning to its vomit or a pig that has been washed returning to roll in mud (2 Pet. 2:20-22).

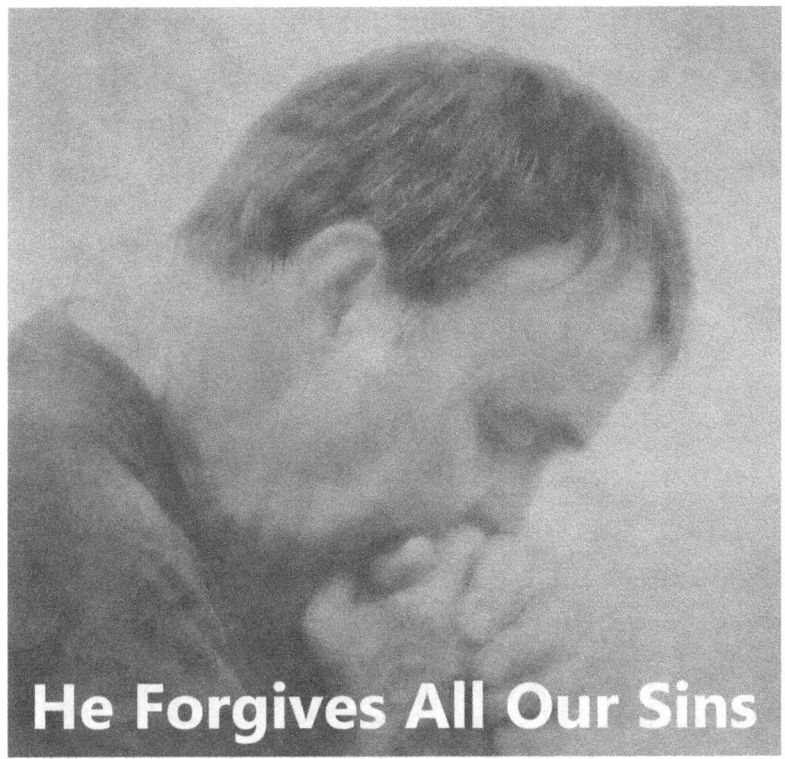

Which of the following names identifies God as the Forgiving God?

A) Yahweh El Nose
B) Yahweh El Elyon
C) Yahweh El Olam
Check answer on Page 78.

14. The God Who Performs

"HE WILL DO WHAT HE HAS PROMISED"

The Bible tells us that God neither sleeps nor slumbers (Psalm 121:4). He is an active God. Jesus said that He does what He sees His Father doing (John 5:19). After healing the man who had been sick for thirty eight years at the pool of Bethesda, Jesus was asked why He had done it on a Sabbath.

He told the Jews that "My Father is always working and I too must work" (GNB John 5:17). In the Old Testament we are told that God confirms the word of His servant and performs the counsel of His messenger (Isaiah 44:26). According to Numbers 23:19, God is certainly going to do what He has said He will do.

Do You Know The Names of God? Part 2

Which of the following names identifies God as the God who performs (does all things for me)?

A) Yahweh El Gomer
B) Yahweh El Shaddai
C) Yahweh Tsebaoth

Check answer on Page 79.

15. The Lord God Of Knowledge

"HE IS ALL KNOWING, ALL WISE"

God knows all things (Job 37:16). He is omniscient. He is the source of all wisdom (James 1:5). Jesus Christ is described as the wisdom of God to believers (1 Cor 1:30). There is nothing that is hidden from God. The secret things belong to God (Deut. 29:29). Christians, who are lacking in wisdom, are called upon to ask God for wisdom for He is willing to supply it generously to all those who ask Him (James 1:5).

There are two kinds of wisdom mentioned in the Bible viz. the wisdom that is "earthly and devilish and full of strife" often referred to as worldly wisdom. Then there is the wisdom that comes from above i.e. divine wisdom (James 3:13-17). The latter is what God wants to supply.

It is personified in James where we are told that it is pure, peaceable, gentle, entreatable (or approachable), full of good fruits, full of mercy, without partiality and without hypocrisy. We can use these attributes to check what kind of wisdom we have.

> O the depth of the riches both of the wisdom and knowledge of God! How unsearchable are His judgments, and His ways past finding out!
> (Romans 11:33)

Romans 11:33 O the depth of the riches both of the wisdom and knowledge of God! How unsearchable are His judgments, and His ways past finding out!.

Which of the following names identifies God as all-knowing?

A) Yahweh Shalom
B) Yahweh El Roi
C) Yahweh El De'ot

Check answer on Page 80.

16. The Lord The Awesome God

"HE IS AWESOME IN TIME & SPACE"

Something is awesome if it inspires an overwhelming feeling of reverence, admiration, fear or awe. God is awesome. When we think of creation, we marvel at His awesomeness. His attention to detail in all of creation is unmatched. All these things did not happen by accident. God is the architect of the universe, both of the things that are seen and those that are not seen. Both spiritual and physical realities were created by Him. He made a way for man's deliverance through His Son, Jesus Christ. The devil thought he had finished man and that man was doomed forever after disobeying God. However, God had prepared a plan for salvation beforehand. God knows all things.

God exists in all space, time and even eternity. He is awesome. The way He delivered the children of Israel from Egypt is also awesome. He parted the Red Sea for them to go through. God can even intervene in the course of nature to answer His servants. Joshua called upon the Sun and the moon to stand still for almost a full day so that Joshua could finish the battle against the Amorites. This is recorded in

Joshua 10:12-14, where the Bible says there has never been such a day before or after.

Nehemiah 1:5 And I said, I pray You, O Jehovah, the God of Heaven, the great and awesome God who keeps covenant and mercy for those who love Him and keep His commandments; (MKJV).

Which of the following names identifies God as the Great, Awesome God?

A) Yahweh El Channun
B) Yahweh Hannorah
C) Yahweh Rapha

Check answer on Page 82.

17. The God of Truth

"HE IS THE WAY, THE TRUTH, THE LIFE"

Jesus said He's the Way, the Truth and the Life (John 14:6). No man comes to the Father except through Him. Nowadays there is a lot of deception. Unfortunately this deception has crept into the church. Jesus said you shall know the Truth and the Truth shall set (make) you free. Jesus came to testify to the truth, God's truth (John 18:37). He prayed for the disciples that the Father may sanctify them with the Truth which is the word of God (John 17:17).

The devil has infiltrated churches. Some men and women of God have started playing with the word of God for one reason or another. Sometimes they may use the word to justify something (a hypothesis) that is not biblical. This is often to further personal (selfish) agenda (Jude 1:3-4).

In theology this is often called eisegesis (not exegesis). Eisegesis is trying to justify something that is not right (true) by distorting the meaning of scripture. Usually, this is done by quoting scripture out of context. Instead of reading meaning from scripture, they read meaning into scripture.

Another strategy is to use just one portion of scripture (often out of context) to justify some notion or action. Jesus warned the Church of those who will come in His name but will be deceivers. Paul wrote and said whoever, whether angel or man, was to preach another gospel was to be cursed (Gal 1:8-9).

All believers should endeavor to study the word of God for themselves (like the Berean church) to verify what they are taught in churches or through the media. God is the absolute Truth, and He has manifested Himself through His Son, Jesus Christ and through the Scripture (the written Word) and through His Holy Spirit.

2 Corinthians 4:2 But we have renounced the hidden things of shame, not walking in craftiness, nor adulterating the Word of God, but by the revelation of the truth commending ourselves to every man's conscience in the sight of God.

Do You Know The Names of God? Part 2

Which of the following names identifies God as the God of Truth?

A) Yahweh Uzzi
B) Yahweh Emeth
C) Yahweh Ori

Check answer on Page 84.

18. The Merciful God

"THE LORD IS FULL OF MERCY"

The Lord God Almighty is merciful. The Bible tells us that His mercies are new every morning (Lamentations 3:22-23). His mercies are tender and His mercies endure or last forever for the people that reverence Him and keep His commandments (Deu. 5:10,Psa. 103:11, 1Ch. 16:34). Though our sins be as red as scarlet, He is always ready to forgive us. However we must come to Him with a repentant heart and ask for forgiveness.

We are not to come arrogantly. He only considers those who come with humility and repentance in their hearts. Some people think that they can sin as much as they want and then ask for forgiveness. God is not mocked; He searches our hearts and judges our motives. No one is smarter than Him.

God is merciful to those who show mercy (Psalm 18:25). In the beatitudes the Bible says, "Blessed are the merciful for they shall obtain mercy" (Matthew 5:7). There is one important condition which God has given for us to enjoy His mercy and forgiveness.

Jesus taught the disciples that they must forgive one another for their sins to be forgiven (Matthew 6:14-15). When people accept Jesus Christ as Lord and Savior and ask to be forgiven of their sins, they must remember to explicitly forgive anyone who has wronged them in their past. They are also supposed to forgive those who will offend them in the future.

Psalm 103:11 For as the heavens are high above the earth, so is His mercy toward those who fear Him.

Do You Know The Names of God? Part 2

Which of the following names identifies God as the Merciful God? (Click the correct answer)

A) Yahweh Megan
B) Yahweh El Chesed
C) Yahweh Ganan

Check answer on Page 85.

19. The God of Compassion

"COMPASSION IS AN EXPRESSION OF LOVE"

Jesus Christ in His earthly ministry was moved with compassion to heal the sick and to deliver the bound. "And Jesus went out and saw a great crowd, and He was moved with compassion toward them. And He healed their sick" (Matt. 14:14). One time, in Jericho, Jesus passed by two blind men who called upon Him to heal them. Jesus had compassion on them, He touched their eyes and they were healed (Matt. 20:30-34).

A leper came to Jesus and asked Him to make him clean. Jesus had compassion on him and healed him (Mark 1:40-41). Jesus' ministry on earth was a manifestation of God's compassion on mankind.

God expects all of us to be compassionate towards one another. Jesus Christ gave a parable of a servant who owed his master, the king, a lot of money. He was to be put in prison for a long time but he begged his master (the king) for mercy. The king was moved with compassion and forgave him everything.

Unfortunately, the servant was not as compassionate. He was owed a small amount money by another servant. The other servant begged him for more time to pay but to no avail. He sent the fellow servant to prison. The other servants reported this unkindness to the king who reversed the earlier decision and handed over the unforgiving servant to be tormented until he paid up everything (Matthew 18:23-35). Jesus reiterated that unless we forgive others, our heavenly Father would also not forgive us.

In Matthew 25:34-35 Jesus gave another example to show the importance of compassion or kindness in the kingdom. Those who inherit the kingdom of God are described as those who bear the fruit of compassion (kindness) by feeding the hungry and thirsty, by caring for strangers, by clothing the poor, by visiting others in hospital or prison, etc.. These will inherit everlasting life.

Those who do not do these things will inherit everlasting punishment. Acts of kindness are not to be confused with the criteria for salvation but one product of salvation. The fruit of the Spirit is love, joy, peace, patience, kindness, goodness, faithfulness, meekness (humility) and self-control (discipline) according to Galatians 5:22.

Do You Know The Names of God? Part 2

Which of the following names identifies God as the God of Compassion?

A) Yahweh El Rachum
B) Yahweh El Berit
C) Yahweh El Shaddai

Check answer on Page 86.

20. The Gracious God

"HE GIVES GRACE TO THE HUMBLE..."

God is very merciful and gracious. There is a difference between grace and mercy. One of the simplest ways of explaining the difference is this. If you forgive someone who has done you some wrong, you have shown mercy. You do not hold their wrong (sin) against them i.e. in your future dealings you do not consider what they did to you to determine your actions towards them.

If you go beyond that and do something good for them, you will be manifesting grace e.g. if you find them sick and take them to hospital or if they are about to lose their house and you pay off their mortgage, etc.

When we receive Jesus Christ as our Lord and Savior, God is merciful to forgive us all our sins and through His grace He ushers into His abundant life (eternal life). We are saved by God's grace (Ephesians 2:8-9). He goes beyond forgiving us and He gives us a new life. He avails to us resources of His kingdom, His blessing, His Holy Spirit and His gifts (of the Holy Spirit), His anointing and empowerment, etc. that we may be fruitful in the work He has called us to do (Ephesians 2:10).

We have access to God's grace through faith in Jesus Christ (Romans 5:2). The grace is for all. Titus 2:11 "For the grace of God that brings salvation has appeared to all men,..." This grace is accessible to the humble (1 Peter 5:5). God's grace is sufficient for us to meet every need in our lives (2 Corinthians 12:9).

Everyone, as a custodian of God's grace, has a gift from God to minister in His body, the Church (1 Peter 4:10). We should beware bitterness. Bitterness is dangerous. It defiles people. If we harbor bitterness in our hearts, we will fall short of the grace of God (Hebrews 12:15).

1 Corinthians 15:10 "But by the grace of God I am what I am, and His grace which was toward me has not been without fruit, but I labored more abundantly than all of them; yet not I, but the grace of God with me".

Which name identifies God as the Gracious God? (Click the correct answer)

A) Yahweh El Elyon
B) Yahweh Hakkadosh
C) Yahweh El Channun

Check answer on Page 87.

Do You Know The Names of God? Part 2

Answers & Prayers Using the Names of God

Answer 1B

Congratulations! That is the right answer:

You can read the following portions of scripture about Yahweh Tsidkenu. (*phonetic pronunciation: tsid-kay'-noo*)

1) God would be called our righteousness in Jesus Christ:

Jeremiah 23:5-6 Behold, the days come, says Jehovah, that I will raise to David a righteous Branch, and a King shall reign and act wisely, and shall do judgment and justice in the earth. (6) In his days Judah shall be saved, and Israel shall dwell safely. And this is His name by which He shall be called, JEHOVAH, OUR RIGHTEOUSNESS. (MKJV)

2) The righteousness of God is upon those who believe in Jesus Christ by faith:

Romans 3:21-26 But now a **righteousness of God** *has been revealed apart from Law, being witnessed by the Law and the Prophets; (22) even the righteousness of God through the faith of Jesus Christ, toward all and upon all those who believe. For there is no difference, (23) for all have sinned and come short of the glory of God, (24) being justified freely by His grace through the redemption that is in Christ Jesus; (25) whom God has set forth to be a propitiation through faith in His blood,* *to declare His righteousness through the passing by of the sins that had taken place before, in the forbearance of God; (26) for the display of His righteousness at this time, for Him to be just and, forgiving the one being of the faith of Jesus.*

3) The righteousness of God is a gift:

*Romans 5:17 For if by one man's offense death reigned by one, much more they who receive abundance of grace and the **gift of righteousness** shall reign in life by One, Jesus Christ.)*

4) We (believers) are the righteousness of God in Jesus Christ:

*2 Corinthians 5:21 For He has made Him who knew no sin, to be sin for us, that we might become the **righteousness of God** in Him.*

You can thank God by saying this short prayer:

Dear loving heavenly Father, Yahweh, I want to thank you today for the gift of righteousness through Jesus Christ, your Son, for I acknowledge Him as my Lord and Savior. Thank You.

Amen

Answer 2C

Congratulations! That is the right answer:

You can read Ezekiel 48:35 about Yahweh Shammah. (*phonetic pronunciation: shawm'-maw*)

It says:

"All around it shall be eighteen thousand cubits. And the name of the city from that day shall be JEHOVAH IS THERE". (MKJV)

You can acknowledge God by saying this short prayer:

Yahweh, I acknowledge that you exist. You are the one who created everything that exists. May you continue to increase me in Your wisdom as I continue to acknowledge You and reverence Your name. I ask this in Jesus name.

Amen

Answer 3A

Congratulations! That is the right answer:

You can read the following portion of scripture about Yahweh Mekaddishkem.

Exodus 31:13

*Speak also to the sons of Israel, saying, Truly you shall keep My sabbaths. For it is a sign between Me and you throughout your generations, to know that I am **Jehovah who sanctifies you**. (MKJV)*

You can thank God by saying this short prayer:

Thank You God (Yahweh) for sanctifying me through the blood of Your Son Jesus Christ. I also thank You for daily sanctifying me through Your Word (Truth) in Jesus name.

Amen.

Answer 4A

Congratulations! That is the right answer:

You can read the following portions of scripture about Yahweh Tsebaoth.

Here are some portions of Scripture:

*1 Samuel 15:2 So says **Jehovah of Hosts**, I will visit Amalek with what he did to Israel, how he set against him in the way when he came up from Egypt.*

*1 Samuel 17:45 And David said to the Philistine, You come to me with a sword and with a spear and with a javelin. But I come to you in the name of **Jehovah of Hosts**, the God of the armies of Israel, whom you have defied.*

*2 Samuel 5:10 And David went on and became great, and Jehovah, the **God of Hosts** was with him. (MKJV)*

You can thank God by saying this short prayer:

I acknowledge you Yahweh as the Lord of the Armies of Heaven. There has never been another like You. There is none like You and there will never be another like You. You are the one who instructs your angels to protect your loved ones. You are my Yahweh Tsebaoth. Thank You in Jesus name. Amen.

Answer 5C

Congratulations! That is the right answer:

You can read the following portions of scripture about Yahweh El Yeshuatenu (The God of our Salvation) or Yahweh El Yeshuati (the God of my Salvation).

*Isa. 12:2 Behold, **God is my salvation**; I will trust and not be afraid for the LORD JEHOVAH is my strength and my song; He also has become my salvation.*

*Psalm 68:19 Blessed is Jehovah; He daily bears burdens for us, the **God of our salvation**. Selah.*

(MKJV)

You can thank God by saying this short prayer:

Thank you God (Yahweh) for being the God of my salvation. I thank You for your plan of salvation through Your Son Jesus Christ whom I acknowledge as my Lord and Savior.

Amen.

Answer 6A

Congratulations! That is the right answer:

You can read the following portion of scripture about Yahweh El Sali.

Psalm 18:2

*Jehovah is my strength, and my fortress, and my deliverer; my God, **my rock**; I will trust in Him; He is my shield, and the horn of my salvation, my high tower. (MKJV)*

Isaiah 26:4

"Trust in the LORD forever, For in GOD the LORD, we have an everlasting Rock".

Other portions of scripture: Psalm 27:5, Psalm 40:2, Isaiah 32:2, Isaiah 44:8, Psalms 71:3

You can acknowledge God by saying this short prayer:

I acknowledge you Yahweh as my Rock. You are my firm foundation. I declare I shall not be moved. I shall abide in You forever in Jesus name.

Amen.

Answer 7C

Congratulations! That is the right answer:

You can read the following portion of scripture about Yahweh Uzzi.

Psalm 28:7 Jehovah is my strength and my shield; my heart trusted in Him, and I am helped; therefore my heart greatly rejoices; and with my song I will praise Him.

Ephesians 6:10 Finally, my brothers, be strong in the Lord and in the power of His might.

You can acknowledge God by saying this short prayer:

I acknowledge you Yahweh Uzzi as my strength. I will always call upon you in times of weakness for you are my strength. I will be strong in You and in the power of Your might in accordance with Your Word in Jesus name.

Amen.

Answer 8C

Congratulations! That is the right answer:

You can read the following portion of scripture about Yahweh Ori.

Psalm 27:1 A Psalm of David. Jehovah is my light and my salvation; whom shall I fear? Jehovah is the strength of my life; of whom shall I be afraid? (MKJV)

You can acknowledge God by saying this short prayer:

I acknowledge you Yahweh as the my Light. Your Word is a lamp to my feet and a light to my path. Make me to walk in Your light always that I may always be in fellowship with You in Jesus name.

Amen.

Answer 9B

Congratulations! That is the right answer:

You can read the following portion of scripture about Yahweh Rabah Sakar (*phonetic pronunciation: Raw-baw' Saw-kawr'*).

*Genesis 15:1 After these things the Word of Jehovah came to Abram in a vision, saying, Fear not, Abram, I am your shield and your exceeding **great reward**. (MKJV)*

You can thank God by saying this short prayer:

I thank You Yahweh Rabah-Sakar for being my exceeding great reward. People may not thank me for what I do. I may not even be appreciated for the work I do voluntarily. I know that you are a righteous judge and the rewarder of those who work tirelessly and selflessly for your Kingdom in Jesus name.

Amen.

Answer 10A

Congratulations! That is the right answer:

You can read the following portions of scripture about Yahweh Maxi (Machsi).

*Psalm 46:1-2 To the Chief Musician. For the sons of Korah. A Song "For the Virgins". God is our **refuge** and strength, a very present help in trouble. (2) Therefore we will not fear when the earth changes, and when mountains are slipping into the heart of the seas.*

*Psalm 91:9-10 Because You, O Jehovah, are My **refuge**; if you have made the Most High your dwelling-place, (10) no evil shall befall you, nor shall any plague come near your dwelling.*

You can thank God by saying this short prayer:

I thank You Yahweh Maxi for being my refuge and dwelling place. In You I live, move and have my being. May it be to me according to Your Word that no evil shall befall me nor any plague come near my dwelling place. I thank You in Jesus name.

Amen.

Answer 11C

Congratulations! That is the right answer:

You can read the following portions of scripture about Yahweh Magen (or Megan). (*phonetic pronunciation: maw-gane'*)

*Psalm 59:11 Do not kill them, lest my people forget; scatter them by Your power and bring them down, O Jehovah our **Shield**.*

*Deuteronomy 33:29 Blessed are you, O Israel! Who is like you, O people saved by Jehovah, the **shield** of your help, and who is the sword of your excellency! And your enemies shall be found liars to you, and you shall tread on their high places.*

You can acknowledge God by saying this short prayer:

I acknowledge You Yahweh Magen, my Shield. You are the One who protects me. My you continue to shield me with your favor as a shield in Jesus name.

Amen.

Answer 12B

Congratulations! That is the right answer:

You can read the following portions of scripture about Yahweh El Malki (my King).

Psalm 68:24 They have seen Your goings, O God; the goings of my God, my King (Yahweh El Malki), in the holy place. (MKJV)

Psalm 98:6 With trumpets and sound of a horn make a joyful noise before Jehovah, the King (Yahweh El Melech).

You can acknowledge God by saying this short prayer:

I acknowledge You Yahweh El Malki. You are my King. You own all that I have. I am only a custodian. I am here to serve my King. It is my privilege to serve you Yahweh El Malki. Grant my the grace to serve you well, in Jesus name.

Amen.

Answer 13A

Congratulations! That is the right answer:

You can read the following portion of scripture about Yahweh El Nose. (*phonetic pronunciation: naw-saw'*)

Psalm 99:8 You answered them, O Jehovah our God; You were a God who forgave them, though You take vengeance for their deeds. (MKJV)

You can acknowledge God by saying this short prayer:

I acknowledge You Yahweh El Nose as the God who forgave me all my sins when I accepted Jesus Christ, your Son, as my Lord and Savior. You also justified me and granted me Your righteousness. Thank You Father in Jesus name.

Amen.

Answer 14A

Congratulations! That is the right answer:

You can read the following portion of scripture about Yahweh El Gomer (*phonetic pronunciation: gaw-mar'*).

Psalm 57:2 I will cry unto God most high; unto God that performeth all things for me.

You can thank God for doing so much for us by saying this short prayer:

I thank You Yahweh El Gomer who has done and continues to do all things for me. On my own, I can do nothing but with You I can do all things.

Amen.

Answer 15C

Congratulations! That is the right answer:

You can read the following portions of scripture about Yahweh El De'ot (the God of Knowledge).

1 Samuel 2:3 Talk no more so very proudly. Remove arrogance out of your mouth, for Jehovah is a God of knowledge, and by Him actions are weighed.

Psalm 147:5 Great is our LORD, and of great power; There is no limit to His understanding.

Job 37:16 Do you know the balancing of the clouds, the wonderful works of Him who is perfect in knowledge?

1 John 3:19-20 And in this we shall know that we are of the truth, and shall assure our hearts before Him, (20) that if our heart accuses us, God is greater than our heart and knows all things.

Hebrews 4:13 Neither is there any creature that is not manifest in His sight, but all things are naked and opened to the eyes of Him with whom we have to do.

(MKJV)

You can acknowledge God as the one who knows everything and ask for wisdom:

Lord, Yahweh El De'ot, I acknowledge you as the all-knowing God. You knew me before I was formed in my mother's womb. You are familiar with all my ways, when I go out and when I return. Your knowledge has no limits and is unsearchable. All things are bare before you. You have invited us to ask You for wisdom. I pray, Abba Father, that you fill me with Your Spirit of wisdom and revelation that I may know all that You want me to know and that I may walk in Your wisdom in accordance with Your Word, in Jesus Christ's name.

Amen.

Answer 16B

Congratulations! That is the right answer:

You can read the following portions of scripture about Yahweh Hannorah.

*Nehemiah 9:32 "Now therefore, our God, the great, the mighty, and the **awesome God**, who keeps covenant and loving-kindness, do not let all the hardship seem insignificant before You, which has come upon us, our kings, our princes, our priests, our prophets, our fathers and on all Your people, from the days of the kings of Assyria to this day..." (NASV)*

*Deuteronomy 10:17, For the LORD your God is the God of gods and the Lord of lords, the great, the mighty, and the **awesome God** who does not show partiality nor take a bribe. (NASV)*

Psalm 89:7 A God greatly feared in the council of the holy ones, and awesome above all those who are around Him? (NASV)

You can acknowledge God's awesomeness in this short prayer:

Abba Father, You are truly awesome. Your ways are above our ways and Your thoughts above our thoughts. You declare the end from the beginning. You do everything according to the counsel of Your own will. Yet Your ear is "open to the prayers" of the righteous. You hear them as they call upon You as Joshua did. May my prayers always be a delight to You. As You sit in Your glorious throne, remember me and consider the meditation of my heart in Jesus Christ's name.

Amen.

Answer 17B

Congratulations! That is the right answer:

You can read the following portion of scripture about Yahweh Emeth.

Psalms 31:5 Into Your hand I commit my spirit; You have redeemed me, O Jehovah, the God of truth (MKJV).

You can acknowledge God as the God of Truth in this short prayer:

Yahweh Emeth, my dear loving heavenly Father, You are the God of Truth. I pray that You sanctify me daily with Your truth, Your word, that I may walk in Your truth always, fully pleasing in Your sight in Jesus name.

Amen.

Answer 18B

Congratulations! That is the right answer:

You can read the following portions of scripture about Yahweh El Chesed.

Psalms 59:10 The God of my mercy shall go before me; God shall let me see my desire on my enemies. (MKJV)

Lamentations 3:22-23 It is of the LORD'S mercies that we are not consumed, because his compassions fail not. (23) They are new every morning: great is thy faithfulness. (KJV)

Psalm 103:11 For as the heavens are high above the earth, so is His mercy toward those who fear Him. (MKJV)

You can acknowledge God who is merciful in this short prayer:

Remember mercy Oh Lord, You are Yahweh El Chesed. I repent of my sins and forgive all those who have offended me. I now ask You to forgive me all my sins in Jesus name.

Amen.

Answer 19A

Congratulations! That is the right answer:

You can read the following portion of scripture about Yahweh El Rachum (*phonetic pronunciation: rakh-oom'*).

Deuteronomy 4:31 For Jehovah your God is a merciful (compassionate) God; He will not forsake you, nor destroy you, nor forget the covenant of your fathers which He swore to them. (MKJV)

Deuteronomy 4:31 For God is compassionate. The LORD your God won't fail you. He won't destroy you or forget the covenant that He confirmed with your ancestors. (ISV)

(Please note the word used in Hebrew is Rachum which means compassionate in English. You can also see Yahweh El Chesed - the God of mercy, in Chapter 18.)

You can acknowledge God as the compassionate God in this short prayer:

Lord, You are Yahweh El Rachum, the compassionate God. Thank You for Your compassion towards me. You expect me to be compassionate towards my neighbors. Grant me the grace to show your compassion to others in Jesus Name. Amen.

Answer 20C

Congratulations! That is the right answer:

You can read the following portion of scripture about Yahweh El Channun (*phonetic pronunciation: khan-noon'*).

Jonah 4:2 And he prayed to Jehovah and said, Please, O Jehovah, was this not my saying when I was still in my land? On account of this I fled before to Tarshish. For I knew that You are a **gracious God,** *and merciful, slow to anger, and of great kindness, and One who repents over calamity. (MKJV)*

You can acknowledge God for His grace in this short prayer:

Yahweh El Channun, I thank You for Your grace that is always sufficient. I am who I am and I can be all that You want me to be by Your grace. I am asking You to continue multiplying your grace in my life that I may live a victorious life and accomplish much more for Your kingdom in Jesus' name.

Amen.

Further Reading

This is Part 2 in the series. If you have not read Part 1, you can get it on Amazon Kindle. Part 2 is also available on Kindle. The Kindle version is interactive. If you get the wrong answer, you are given another chance to state the right name of God in the quiz. If you get it right you are allowed to proceed to the next chapter. This makes it easy to remember the Hebrew attribute names of God.

More descriptive names of God (YHWH) will be available in Part 3.

If you would like more information about Part 3; you can email the author at abouthashem@gmail.com

About the Author

Paul Muinde loves studying God's word, singing His praises and sharing His word with others. Paul believes that the body of Christ needs daily edification. Believers should build each other in the faith through reading and applying God's word.

Believers should also worship God through psalms and spiritual songs and pray always for God's will to be done on the earth as it is done in Heaven. Paul was a member of the advisory board of a local church for many years where he was better known as Elder Shalom. He is currently pastoring a local church with his wife Rose in Kenya.

www.ingramcontent.com/pod-product-compliance
Lightning Source LLC
LaVergne TN
LVHW011736060526
838200LV00051B/3190